NIGHT HOLDS ITS OWN

POEMS

CIARA SHUTTLEWORTH

BLUE HORSE PRESS REDONDO BEACH, CALIFORNIA   2016

NIGHT HOLDS ITS OWN

CIARA SHUTTLEWORTH

Blue Horse Press
P.O. Box 7000 - 760
Redondo Beach,
California   90277

Copyright © 2016 by Ciara Shuttleworth.
All rights reserved.
Printed in the United States of America.

Cover art: "Valentine's Day"
by Ciara Shuttleworth
Model credit: Shawn Erin Cardwell

Editors: Jeffrey and Tobi Alfier
Blue Horse Press logo: Amy Lynn Hayes

ISBN 978-0692636336

Acknowledgments

Some of these poems first appeared in the following journals and anthologies: *Alaska Quarterly Review* ("Long Distance"); *Cascadia Review* ("Theory and Practice"); *Confrontation* ("Vacant as the Sky"); *Crab Creek Review* ("I've Written You a Sunset"); *Cutthroat* ("Seduction"); *Los Angeles Review* ("What Sings Is the Drunk Boy's Hands"); *Minnetonka Review* ("Independence Day" in an earlier version, and "The Moon's Silence"); *The New Yorker* ("Sestina"); *The Norton Introduction to Literature, 11/e* ("Sestina"); *Ploughshares* ("Limerence"); *The Practice of Creative Writing: A Guide for Students, 2/e & 3/e* ("Sestina"); *Slipstream* ("Electric like Lightning"); *The Southern Review* ("Deck of Hearts" and "Highway"); *Tahoma Literary Review* ("Conductive Hearing"); *Thrush* ("Fuck Broken Dishes" and "Waiting for Nothing"); *Tule Review* ("Love's Cartographers" and "Words like Fire"); and *Weber: the Contemporary West* ("Night Holds Its Own").

"Sestina" was used in *Sestina*, Judah Adashi's composition for Voice and Orchestra, performed at Carnegie Hall on October 23, 2015, by the American Composers Orchestra and sung by Pulitzer Prize-winner Caroline Shaw. "Sestina" was also performed as part of *Six (6)* by Frank Pesci at the Trinity Church in Boston on November 13, 2011.

Many thanks to Jeff and Tobi Alfier.

Special thanks to Bob Wrigley, Mary Blew, Terri Gaffney, Sonya Dunning, Ian Segal, and Judah Adashi.

I am particularly grateful to The Kerouac Project of Orlando and the Orlando writing community for three beautiful months at the Kerouac House—especially Danielle Kessinger, Summer Rodman, and Jack Kerouac's lingering ghost.

For Luke, skittish hopeless romantic, my misguided angel, my brother. And for my parents and sisters: Red, Kate, Mo, and Jessi: with all my love and thanks for the years, the miles, the support.

Table of Contents

Eventually, Soon	1
Independence Day	2
I've Written You a Sunset	4
The Moon's Silence	5
Fuck Broken Dishes	7
Sestina	9
Conductive Hearing	11
Night Holds Its Own	12
Vacant as the Sky	13
Highway	14
Deck of Hearts	15
What Sings Is the Drunk Boy's Hands	16
Seduction	18
Electric like Lightning	19
Words like Fire	20
Long Distance	21
Limerence	22
Love's Cartographers	23
Theory and Practice	24
Waiting for Nothing	25
Harnessing Electricity	27

...but the rain
is full of ghosts tonight...
— Edna St. Vincent Millay

Eventually, Soon

If you believe there is no beginning

or end, no ceiling
or ground to contain us, that we may float

and nest like birds in the in-between,
the dust on moth wings

as dirty as it gets, then you must forget.

Forget the accumulation
of artifacts and wrinkles, forget

the dead roses in the vase
so that you might throw them away

without guilt. Take these first few days
recklessly, as you must, but know that all you promise

has been drawn up, a contract
unwritten yet signed. You know

when I turn to you it is in search
of the joy I held when you flew after me.

Maybe that's about the time you start thinking
that when love gets too heavy

you've got to lay it down. Because you know

that when I turn from you
I am seeking the same flight.

Independence Day

I'm concentrating on the rearview
like I'm going somewhere,
like I don't feel like touching up my life
with a tire iron, like I meant to break
every firecracker dish or glass
for the beauty of it only, and only for you.

It's the Fourth of July
and there's a girl on the corner,
nutra-sweet skinny with black hair and black pants.
The light's fading
but I know she's waiting, like me,
for it all to blow her away.

I don't have to look through your window
or lean against your doorframe to know
you're already asleep. If I jumped off
this alley into your dreams, you'd sleep on.

Fourth of July and there's a blanket over a stop sign,
hanging askew,
a glowing ice sculpture in headlights.
Caution: Iceberg Ahead.

I'll still be sizzling when the sun rotates back
toward our sky, pulling you with it, to stand.
I'll hand you coffee and cross my legs like a prom queen.
I'll say *You're going about this like a used car salesman,
telling me to hitch-hike blue skies.*
I'll take your silence for response.
I'll unravel
the fuse and coax it into flame.
I'll say *Boom.*

I've Written You a Sunset

You park on the curb of my heart
    never come in

        just rev your engine
like I've been waiting primped and perfumed by the mirror

but I'm not here for your test drive hit and run
    I want it all in writing

        because I don't believe
    a word you're breathing

down my neck

You bought your heart from a street vendor

and who cares if

I've spent hours crafting
    canny dialogue
when you never get your lines right

but the sky is smoothing

so here's your out:

The Moon's Silence

The moon asks nothing more
than to be full once a month,

so I'll wait for morning
when I can share lies with the crow outside my window—

anyone can be angry enough to disappear. Even the moon
leaves us in dark one night a month.

I take a taxi and pretend I'm in a movie:
I'm in the backseat, the bass of the soundtrack

pulsing through my hands, shifting
my destination from nowhere, fast.

I tell the driver, *just keep driving, drive
all night, windows down.*

The moon slips in, sits beside me
like someone I could call a friend.

What I want is sunrise
tasting like kisses, grapefruit-red

and caught on an incoming tide….reckless
promises I intend to keep. I'm not ready

to face the dark alone.
And neither is the moon, the Hollywood starlet

who rarely shows her face before dinner,
but we know when she swoons from the sky

it's not suicide, just a plea we don't forget her.

Fuck Broken Dishes

once you've seen what wine glasses
can do to a face,
what you can do with silk and lace
to suffocate the one you love
so much you want them glove
close, always in sight,
like you don't breathe right
when they are near or when they
are as far as the memory of Sunday
mass. Fuck cold-

cock punches, I'm the one holding
the throwing fist, no restraint,
the heat,
my vision red
until he can hold me anchored
and we play makeup sex,
pretend the effects
of me plus him in such potency
will calm. Nobody
will tell him to stay, not me.
I want to beat him until he bleeds,
bleed until I feel life
flow into me, the penultimate fight:
beat rather than be
beaten. But he never raises a fist to me.
Never raises his voice or closes

doors between us. The mirror exposes
something shattered, waiting, silent.
The longer I look, the more I find
the next thing I break will be
me.

Sestina

You
used
to
love
me
well.

Well,
you—
me—
used
love
to…

to…
well…
love.
You
used
me.

Me,
too,
used…
well…
you.
Love,

love
me.
You,
too

well
used,

used
love
well.
Me,
too.
You!

You used
to love
me well.

Conductive Hearing

You wait and it doesn't come back.
Somewhere not too far north, a train derails.
You're still listening for the sound
of a fog horn, think it was a dream,
your imagination, a semi. Maybe.
Or maybe you heard the train slip the track on a curve,
still three miles north, and since you weren't
paying attention, and since the shriek of metal and mouths
had to shiver through tunnels
and rain and wind pushing back against it,
can anyone blame you
for mistaking your loneliness for the ocean?
The train curled like you on its side, ground-facing
ditch light blown, the other a beacon
toward the sun. The lone headlight
shines down a day-lit track.

Night Holds Its Own

even on the darkest roads east of town
where precious stones are still forming
under the earth.

This is where it doesn't matter
if your dreams have become twisted
with the actual—no one can hear your mutterings
and howls. The moon floats
close enough to show you
its mottled surface, always full,
and the water, so pure, cures
your sour stomach, your shaky restless binges.

Under a copse of distant maples,
rumbling tumblers darker than your mind,
motorcycles gun their hope for chaos
down the streets, and sirens widow-wail
on the move.

Rattle of night animals in branches, summer
resuscitates, finally,
prisms across your tongue.

Vacant As the Sky

Lightning to the north, a sky
neoned purple, then rain. Wait.
Don't go in yet. Not until the light burns
your eyes. Then, lonely on your back
on a hotel bed in the same town
where you began, blinded but still watching
clearly the memories of a life
you'll never reclaim, swingsets
and sun, then sunsets and wine,
then just swinging, you'll motion
toward the television as if
in conversation, as if all your old friends
are contained in that box. What was it the lightning saw
—or you saw in it?

                Body of heat, of light, of boozy hues,
strike here first. Take his mind and all
that is in it. Let him start again
with slurred words and crossed
eyes, jittering electric and close
to celestial with emptiness.

Highway

The angle of the sun setting says winter.
Ice on the blacktop reflects headlights,
moonlight. What pauses roadside
eyeglints, tempts anyone alone
to follow its animal scent to a warm den,
to primal tendencies—teeth-snapping
fights for territory, pack, bad meat
swallowed with gravel, bone. To a scavenger's
need to press forward, howling.

Deck of Hearts

What do people mean when they say, *in my heart of hearts*____? Is that like how my brother explained to my neighbor, Anne, that he has dozens of roles women play in his life, but sleeping with him was not *her* role? Nobody has more than one heart, so perhaps they are talking about a deck of cards and maybe the Three of Hearts is their heart of hearts—some amateur version of tarot reading, some lucky poker winner. My brother gave her a brotherly hug, told her he wasn't Mr. Right or even Mr. Right Now but let her sleep off her drunk on his couch cuddling his dog. She was certain he was her King of Hearts and showed up the next night with her guitar, her hair and makeup close to beautiful and still she was not his Four-the-Night of Hearts. Maybe his heart of hearts was the Ace he carried in his wallet, the Glock he kept loaded under his pillow, the butane smell as he burned the deck, got out of this town, not to somewhere better—just *got out*, that Ace of Hearts he'd shuffled back into the deck burned, too, and now his heart of hearts is ash and who knows what happened to Anne and her guitar. Who knows what goes through his mind now as my brother searches for hearts at the casino/bowling alley where he mixes drinks for the entire deck, the Four-the-Nights and Queens he keeps neatly stacked across the bar, none of them Hearts.

What Sings Is the Drunk Boy's Hands

What sings is the drunk boy's hands,
white against the door frame, his hips

dancing without permission, trying
to take flight. Imagine

how his hands must sing
a different song, sang it last night,

sliding like syrup across her body
as she buzzed him in, how his hands held

a yellow tulip, still a bud, like a microphone,
like her, his lover, but her hands lay still.

They did not sing back. Imagine his hands
couldn't stop singing, though he pleaded,

and she turned away, wouldn't
see them. But when she saw his body dance,

possessed by the near-whisper of those fingers,
she knew those hands would sing for anyone,

anywhere. She threw the drunk boy's hands
out on the street, and the drunk boy had no choice

but to follow. What sings is the drunk boy's hands,
hinged white against the door frame, his hips

dancing without permission as he lifts
a knee once, and again, against the glass,

an attempt at entry he has no key
to accomplish. When he gives in, head resting

on shoulder, it is his hands that steady, that lead him
back to the sidewalk—hands like great pink flamingo

heads, arms curving like necks,
the skittering jitterbug of his body trying

to find flight, the drunk boy's hands
always singing, *One more, just one more...*

Seduction

The tang of all that waits and was
my years on water
comes now, inland, land-bound
but flowing, a luminous dark punched open
by full moon, the caress of saltwater on the air
like kisses. I cannot eat
oysters for the reek of ocean,
the million souls sighing, reaching
toward land. It is the smell
that clings to swimmers, the song
calling them back to arms angling
not to pull them under, but to clutch and be carried
to the sand.
                        What became of the girl
who loved there, combing the beach
for whole sand dollars, for driftwood to whittle
into dreams? If I had stayed
I would be keening
with the gulls, reaching into the arms
of the incoming tide, searching for one hand
to form, to grasp back in the frigid saltwater.

Electric like Lightning

I want to feel electric, high voltage, my body
housing unharnessed megawatts equal to a single shard
of lightning, because most days I am a copper wire
bundled with many in a great machine, tarnished
to green as the magnets whirl their great energy
through us, the mineral oil we bathe in dirty and leaking
from the tank. Together we send five-hundred-thousand megawatts through each line out, powering the world
in a way we cannot convince lightning to do. Our current
is direction we do not dictate, have no choice
but to run *this* course, to diverge only when told,
or by happy accident. If not to be lightning, than I wish
to be soaked by rain and out in the open during a lightning
storm so the electricity runs over my body, no jolt or burning
of organs, no frying of the eyes and brain, only this: the ozone
smell that lingers for weeks, will not be washed away.
And this: rawness of the skin when touched, the memory
of all that purple light surrounding me like a veil. *Home*
something escaped into rather than from. Body as *home*
and what grace I'd finally realize,
each breath perfect, each step taking me closer
to the unknown, each dream of purple sky, rain.

Words like Fire

I'm through wondering
how many quarters it's going to take

until I hear your voice   I'm stooped

beneath the street light
scrabbling for a pen to scrawl on any scrap
      so I can warm my hands over the words
words that mean *I'm sorry* in a way
that brings your voice again

saying *Hey baby come 'ere*

Long Distance

                      You ask me
can I see it. As if. As if I can see through
phone lines and satellites. As if I can hold
your hand in one of mine
and a glass of something red in the other.
As if I can look through all the clouds
and light my sky holds to your dark
one, moonlit, full.

Limerence

It is the train-off-a-cliff courting,
the half-mast
eyes across a room, fingers
lingering too long
on the exchange of a book, a cigarette,
an apple. Nights of seeing a face
in the moon and finally
leaving the window to walk empty
dawn streets in search
of a rock or flower to hold
in your pocket for luck. The first taste
of the other's skin, nervous-sweat
turning to embrace, to underwear
accidentally left
between sheets, to cloudy days
almost too bright to endure
and the indulgence
of secrets, to four-letter words
you can never take back
and no matter how many times
you've said them before or will say them again
—to lovers, past and future—
they feel like honey
dripping from your lips
every time, honey
gliding over both your bodies
until you glow, honey,
the only sustenance
you'll ever know.

Love's Cartographers

Life work passed hand to hand, each layer
built upon the luck or curse
of the generation before, secrets held by skin,
lips, loins, years and memory faltering
before taking up the pen to record
the route taken—myth or truth—and a path
sought by the next
set of hands, pen barely skimming the surface
of the page, each fleeting mark spreading
into aged-heavy cotton bond, stronger strokes
leaving ridges and gashes. When a bead
of sweat or tear smudges a line between
terrain, the paper lifts in a welt like new land
rising through fog.

Theory and Practice

The waves are writing a love letter
in cursive, alluring,
while kayaks skim bright exclamation points
and crab boats slur a circle of misspelled words. They pull
from the depths synonyms for love in their wire cages:
look at this nourishment, look at these
armored bodies; stoke the fire and boil to break.

This gift, repetition: waves through the gray,
keeping time, churning toward the dunes.

Waiting for Nothing

There is no time for this
or much of anything else.

Angle down the street
and you'll get a few sideways looks, too.
Raise your hand in hello
as if you know someone,
merge with the crowd
and they'll forget.

Light through my wine glass leaves
a red prism across the book
I meant to read
before steps on the stairs
did not attach to a knock
at my door. No, waiting
for nothing is never dull.

If you sit through the credits, the theater
will empty to the ones unwilling
or –able to go home, their faces
mad with concentration, like maybe
they know a minor gaffer or composer,
like they want to be alone and this
is as close as they ever get.

Me? I hide
in my closet like a child, cedar boards
cool against my legs, and party dresses
brush their gauze against my face, and I believe
again in dancing, although I haven't
in years—or days…time seeps in and out
of clocks too smoothly to tell.

I sidle down the street, angling
               the wrong way through
after work foot traffic.
I raise my hand in hello to no one
and merge with the crowd. They think
I know someone. They think
I'm done waiting. They stare
sideways like presidents on money.
They move on.

Harnessing Electricity

Sky thrown open and the night's electricity
pounds into you. What is left:
bones hollowed to bird-lightness, muscle
and blue veins rumbling against skin.
Flight. The hundreds of miles of oasis
on desert highways. Wear your white dress
but not for any church bell. The rain
will streak the dirt into a roadmap
of where to next.

About the Author

Ciara Shuttleworth was born in San Francisco and grew up in Nebraska, Nevada, and Washington state. Her poetry has been published in journals and anthologies, including *Alaska Quarterly Review*, *Confrontation*, *The New Yorker*, *The Norton Introduction to Literature 11e*, *Ploughshares*, and *The Southern Review*. Shuttleworth received an MFA in poetry from University of Idaho, a BFA in painting/drawing from San Francisco Art Institute, and a BA in studio art from Gustavus Adolphus College. She was a 2014 Jerome Foundation Fellow at the Anderson Center at Tower View, and The Jack Kerouac Project of Orlando's 51st resident at Jack Kerouac House. Her website is www.ciarashuttleworth.com.

www.ingramcontent.com/pod-product-compliance
Lightning Source LLC
Chambersburg PA
CBHW061348040426
42444CB00011B/3142